A Wooden Chair

Sarah Ridley

W

FRANKLIN WATTS
LONDON · SYDNEY

First published in 2005 by
Franklin Watts
96 Leonard Street
London
EC2A 4XD

Franklin Watts Australia
45-51 Huntley Street
Alexandria, NSW 2015

© Franklin Watts 2005

ISBN 0 7496 6063 5
Dewey classification number: 684.1'3

Series editor: Sarah Peutrill
Art director: Jonathan Hair
Design: Jemima Lumley
Photography: Andy Crawford
Picture credits: Argus/Still Pictures: 29c. Digital Vision: front
cover cl. Mary Evans Picture Library: 10br. Nick
Hawkes/Ecoscene: 29t. Hulton-Deutsch/Corbis: 13t. S.J.
Krasemann/Still Pictures: 8b. Robert Maass/Corbis: 28t. Frank
Pedrick/Image Works/Topham: 5tr. Picturepoint/Topham: 30,
31cl. A. Riedmiller/Still Pictures: 4b. Ann Ronan/HIP/Topham:
21b. Ronald Sheridan/Ancient Art & Architecture Collection: 7t.
Paul A. Souders/Corbis: 5cl. Every attempt has been made to
clear copyright. Should there be any inadvertent omission
please apply to the publisher for rectification.

A CIP catalogue record for this book is available from the
British Library.

The author and publisher would like to thank J.K Bone Ltd,
London, and Dylan Pym for their help with this book.

Printed in Malaysia

Contents

The wood for this chair came from a beech tree.

A chair is a piece of furniture for sitting on. Follow the story to see how this chair was made. It has a strong back and arms to rest on. Not all chairs have arms, and the design of chairs can be very different.

▲ The finished chair seat has a comfortable leather pad. This is called upholstery.

➤ Beech trees grow tall and straight, creating good wood for furniture makers.

A lumberjack cuts down the tree. The logs are taken to a sawmill on a truck or train, or floated down a river.

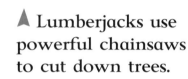
▲ Lumberjacks use powerful chainsaws to cut down trees.

At the sawmill, huge saws cut the logs into long planks.

▲ The sawmill is often close to areas of woodland or forestry.

The planks need to be dried out. Beech wood is kilned, which means it is dried in a heated shed.

Why use wood?

Wood is easy to cut and shape. Some wood has a strong pattern or a dark colour. Other wood is light in colour or even red. Wood can be hard or soft. Some woods bend, while others do not. People can make many styles of chair from the different types of wood.

The chair maker decides what type of chair to make.

Chair makers often choose a chair design from a pattern book. The book contains designs that have already been drawn up. Sometimes a new design is needed and this is drawn on paper, or designed on a computer.

The chair maker has chosen beech wood for this chair. The timber merchant sells the planks to the chair maker. They arrive by van or lorry.

▲ The planks are stacked in a wood store until they are needed.

In the past

Apart from thrones for very important people, the earliest seats were stools and benches. After 1500CE the design of chairs began to develop, until chairs became common in most homes. Amazingly, the ancient Egyptians knew how to make chairs as we know them thousands of years earlier. Some of their chairs have survived because they were buried in the tombs of kings and princes.

This throne is over 3,300 years old. It was found in the tomb of Tutankhamun (ruler of ancient Egypt, c.1361-1352BCE). Under the decoration it is just like a modern chair.

▲ The chair is being made in a small workshop. Today, however, many chairs are made in big factories.

The long planks of wood are taken into a workshop to be cut up. A team of three workers will transform them into a finished chair.

The chair maker cuts up the planks.

The chair maker guides the planks under a bandsaw. He cuts them into roughly the width he wants.

◄▲ The bandsaw is powered by electricity. A sharp blade moves up and down.

Planks cut from wood at the centre of the tree trunk are the strongest.

Why use wood?

Wood is very strong. This is because it is made up of many long threads, called fibres. Wood is cut along the grain - up the length of the fibres. Woodworkers learn which planks of wood to use for each job.

The short lengths of wood are taken to a machine called a planer. This does two jobs. It shaves off the rough top layer of wood to leave it smooth. Then it slices off layers of wood until the plank is the correct thickness.

◀ The chair maker uses the planer to smooth and thin each plank. The tube behind sucks the sawdust away.

▶ A plank of wood before (top) and after (bottom) it has been planed. The planed piece is ready for the next stage.

The chair maker cuts the planks to the exact width.

To do this the chair maker uses a circular saw. It, too, is powered by electricity.

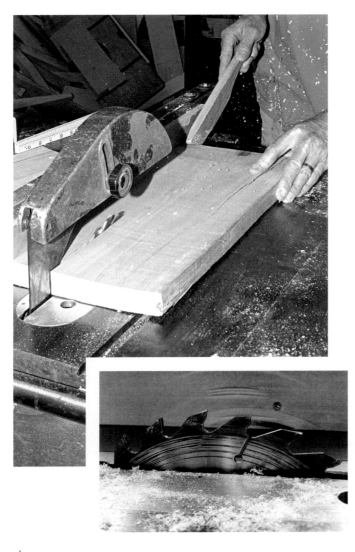

▲ The sharp blades of the circular saw spin round quickly, to cut along the wood.

In the past

Surnames give clues to the jobs that our ancestors did. Sawyer, Turner, Joiner, Carver and Carpenter are all surnames of people whose ancestors probably worked with wood. The sawyer cut up wood, the turner shaped wood, the joiner made windows, staircases and doors, the carver decorated wood and the carpenter did the woodwork on houses.

A 17th-century woodcut showing two carpenters.

Now the chair maker marks out each piece with a template. There is a template for all of the pieces needed to make the chair. A template makes sure that all the chairs will be the same size and shape.

▼ The chair maker is making more than one of this chair, so here he uses a pen to draw around one template piece several times, to save time.

Back leg template

◄ ▲ These are two pieces of the template. The pieces are made from plywood so they won't bend out of shape.

Back support template

The chair maker cuts out the legs, seat and back pieces.

The chair maker carefully guides the bandsaw blade along the pen marks. It is important that all the pieces are cut out accurately as they will have to fit together like a jigsaw puzzle.

Each piece is outlined in pen

➤ It only takes a few minutes to cut out each piece.

In the past

For hundreds of years, apart from a few water-powered sawmills, all wood had to be cut by hand saws. From about 1850, different machines were made to help furniture makers. This meant they could produce decorated furniture much more quickly and at a lower price.

This photograph shows wood workers in 1940 using the old saw-pit method to saw wood. It requires perfect balance and great strength.

▲ Seat pieces are stacked in the workshop.

All the different pieces - for the chair's back legs, seat and back frame - are cut out. The chair maker uses a fret saw for very close cutting.

Because the chair maker is making more than one chair he has to cut out several of each part. They are stacked up together until all the different pieces are cut out.

The chair maker makes connecting joints.

Tenon

Two pieces of wood can be joined together with screws or glue. Chair makers also cut the wood into special shapes that fit together tightly to form joints. Our chair maker creates shapes called mortises and tenons.

A tenon saw is set up to cut away the outside section of the wood to leave the inner tenon.

▲► Once the tenon saw has been set up, it cuts the tenon automatically. The chair maker just has to press a button.

Each tenon will fit into a slot called a mortise. This is the strongest way of joining two pieces of wood.

The chair maker makes the slots. First he puts a leg piece in a mould, called a former. Pen marks show exactly where the slots will be drilled. The former goes under the drill which cuts right through the wood.

▼ To make the chairs quickly, many tenoned pieces are made at once.

Tenon

Former

Drill

▲ The drill has controls that can be set to cut just where it is needed.

Mortise

▲ Slots are needed at the ends and centre of each leg piece.

Why use wood?

Wood can be joined together with many different kinds of joint. To fix the joint really strongly, a hole can be drilled into the joint pieces to fit a wooden peg or, more often today, a metal screw.

The chair maker decorates the back pieces.

The back of the chair is made from four pieces. First a line of holes is drilled into the top back piece.

Then another chair maker carefully marks neat squares around the holes.

◀ Holes are drilled.

Back piece

▼ The squares are marked out in pen.

She uses a chisel and hammer to make the square holes.

Hammer   Chisel

◀ A clamp (at the bottom of the picture) holds the wood steady as the hammer and chisel are used to make the squares.

Next, she puts glue in all the holes. Finally, she pushes small squares of walnut wood into place. This is called inlay.

A machine called a spindle carves grooves into the pieces that will form the lower back support. It would take much longer to do all the grooves by hand.

▶ All the walnut pieces are lined up next to the holes that they will fit into.

Squares of walnut wood

Cutter

▲ This is a finished back support piece. A small tool called a cutter makes the grooves when it is attached to the spindle.

Decorating wood

As well as using inlay and carving, wood furniture can be decorated in many other ways. Veneer is when a thin sheet of a beautifully patterned wood is glued onto another wood. Marquetry is similar but uses thin pieces of veneer of different woods to build up a design or picture.

This beautiful chair from the 17th century has been decorated with both marquetry and carving.

All the pieces are sanded smooth.

Another chair maker uses a belt sander to sand some of the pieces. It is dusty work so he wears a mask. Other parts of the chair are sanded smooth with a hand sander.

▼ The sander machine has a revolving belt of sandpaper. The chair maker presses each piece of wood onto the sandpaper using a sanding pad.

Sanding pad   Wood piece   Belt of sandpaper

The chair is now ready to be put together. Some pieces slot into place, others peg together. The chair makers also use glue to hold the joints firmly.

Three lower back pieces are inserted into a back leg. Then the top piece goes into its mortise slot. Finally, the second leg joins at the other side and the back of the chair is complete.

▲ You can see how the tenoned end of the back piece slots into the mortise slot on the leg.

Decorated top piece

◄ Six pieces of wood are joined together to form the completed back piece.

This section has three lower back pieces

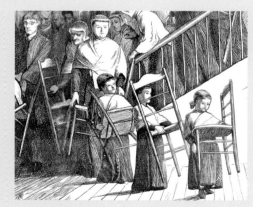

The Shakers lived in a community where they shared everything. Their ladderback chairs reflect their simple lives.

In the past

Certain chair designs are linked to the craftsmen that made them. The Shakers, a religious group, sailed from England to the USA in the mid-18th century. They had a tradition of simple well-crafted chair designs, which continue to be made today. Their belief that God would notice poor workmanship meant that their chairs were beautifully made.

The chair maker joins the rest of the chair.

The laminated arm and leg pieces and the seat frame are glued and slotted together.

The chair maker hammers pegs into the holes at the end of each of the arms and the frame for the seat.

▲ The front part of the chair, including the arms and seat base, is left to dry.

Peg

◄ The pegs are wedged into each hole. Together with the glue, they will hold the chair together strongly.

It is finally time to join the front and back of the chair together.

The chair maker puts glue into each hole and gently eases the chair together.

▼ Glue goes in the holes first, to help the pegs stay in place.

▲ The chair maker works quickly to join the front and back parts of the chair together, before the glue dries.

Flat-packed furniture

Not all chairs are finished off like this one. To make wooden furniture available to everyone, modern furniture factories use cheap wood to make flat-packed furniture. This means that all the pieces of the chair or table are boxed up, with pre-drilled holes and a bag of metal screws. This saves money as the furniture is easy to store and deliver, and it is the customer who spends their own time putting the furniture together.

The chair maker puts on clamps.

The chair is put on its feet. Clamps
hold the chair together until it is dry.

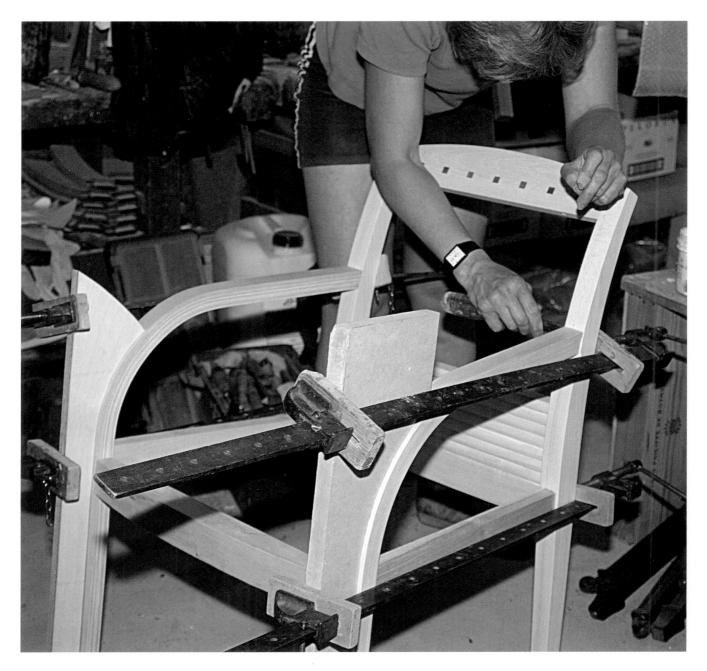

The clamps press all the
glued joints together.

After five minutes, the clamps are taken off. Now angled supports are screwed in place on the chair to create supports for the seat base.

As far as this workshop is concerned the chair is now completed. The customer finishes the chair by varnishing, staining, or waxing it and adding upholstery (padding).

Seat supports

◄ ▲ The seat pad will rest on the chair frame and supports.

Why use wood?

Wood is a useful material when it comes to finishing the chair. The same chair can be made to look quite different. It can be waxed, varnished, painted, oiled or stained to make it lighter or darker. The seat, and sometimes the seat back, can be upholstered with various materials or woven with rushes. If it is looked after properly, wood looks good for hundreds of years.

This chair was made in the 19th century. Nearly all of it has been upholstered.

How a chair is made

It takes two days to transform the planks of wood into a finished chair.

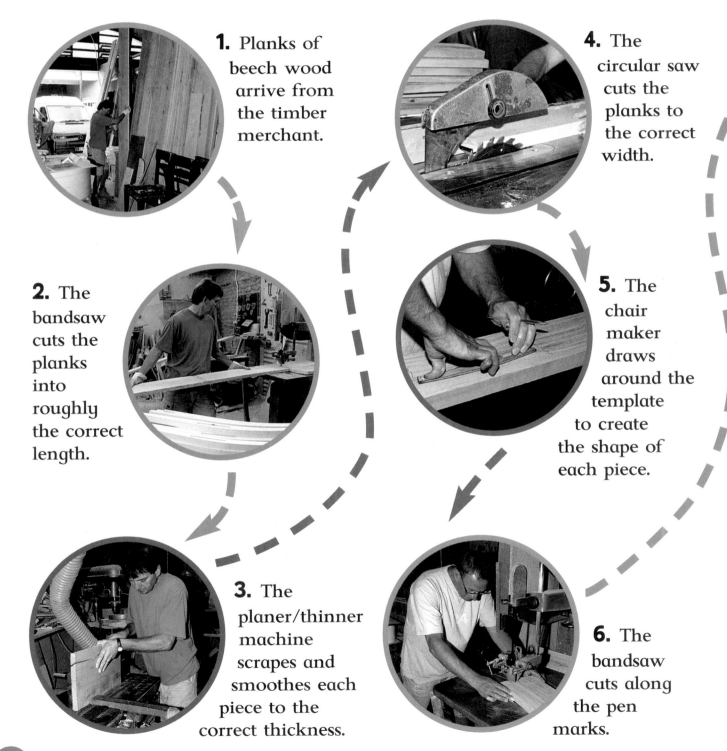

1. Planks of beech wood arrive from the timber merchant.

2. The bandsaw cuts the planks into roughly the correct length.

3. The planer/thinner machine scrapes and smoothes each piece to the correct thickness.

4. The circular saw cuts the planks to the correct width.

5. The chair maker draws around the template to create the shape of each piece.

6. The bandsaw cuts along the pen marks.

7. Mortise and tenon joints are created on some pieces of wood.

11. All the pieces are joined together.

8. The arm and front leg pieces are bent into shape.

12. The chair is ready to be varnished and upholstered.

9. The back piece is decorated.

10. The belt sander makes every piece smooth.

13. The finished chair.

Other uses for wood

People use wood to make many everyday items. A great deal of wood is used to build homes - in window frames, doors, roofs and floors. Then, of course, there is all the furniture - tables, chairs, beds and bookshelves.

Wood can be carved, bent and hammered together to make musical instruments, sculptures and toys. It can even be pulped to make paper! How many things can you think of that are made from wood?

Wood and the environment

Trees are a renewable material. This means that as long as we replant the woodland and forest that we cut down, there will be wood to use in the future.

Sustainable forestry

The worldwide demand for wood is huge. This has led to the destruction of many forests. International organisations are working to encourage good forest management. This is called sustainable forestry. Wood from sustainable forests comes with the FSC (Forest Stewardship Council) mark.

Encourage your family to buy wood and wooden furniture that has this mark.

Rotting away

Wood eventually rots away, unlike many materials. Old wood can be reduced to wood chips for gardens or playgrounds.

All sorts of chairs

Once all chairs were made of wood, but today other materials are available.

From around 1900, chair designers started to play around with both the shape of the chair, and the material it was made from.

Today chairs are made from wood, plastic, leather, metal, fabric and wicker, or a combination of more than one material.

Which of these chairs do you like best?

► This unusual chair was designed by a Spanish architect called Antonio Gaudi in 1900. Gaudi designed the chair to fit the style of the building it was made for. It is made from oak wood and leather.

To break away from the idea that all chairs need four legs, Eero Saarinen designed the Tulip Chair in 1957. It consists of a plastic coated aluminium base topped with a moulded plastic seat.

Chairs can be made from wicker. A frame is made from beech or metal and then split cane and ratan are woven around the frame to create a chair.

Tubular steel is another modern material used to make chairs.

Word bank

Forestry An area of land where trees are planted and cared for by foresters.

Former A mould used to shape wood.

Inlay To set pieces of one type of wood into another type of wood so that they form a decorative flat surface.

Joint The place where two parts fit together.

Laminate To stick layers of wood on top of each other to form a block.

Mortise A slot or hole in a piece of wood that fits a tenon on another piece of wood to form a joint.

Template A shape used as a guide to cut out the sections of a piece of furniture.

Tenon The end of a piece of wood which fits into a mortise on another piece of wood to form a joint.

Upholstery The stuffing, springs and material used to make padded furniture.

Index